Date Due

HUGH WALPOLE
An Appreciation
JOSEPH HERGESHEIMER

BOOKS BY HUGH WALPOLE

NOVELS
- THE WOODEN HORSE
- MR. PERRIN AND MR. TRAILL
- THE GREEN MIRROR
- THE DARK FOREST
- THE SECRET CITY

ROMANCES
- THE PRELUDE TO ADVENTURE
- FORTITUDE
- THE DUCHESS OF WREXE
- MARADICK AT FORTY

BOOKS ABOUT CHILDREN
- THE GOLDEN SCARECROW
- JEREMY

BELLES-LETTRES
- JOSEPH CONRAD: A CRITICAL STUDY

HUGH WALPOLE

HUGH WALPOLE

An Appreciation

by

JOSEPH HERGESHEIMER

Author of "Three Black Pennys"
"Java Head", etc.

*Together with Notes
and Comments on the Novels of
Hugh Walpole*

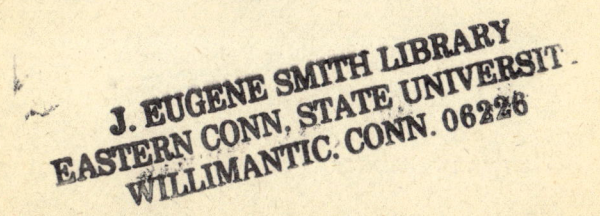

NEW YORK
GEORGE H. DORAN COMPANY

Copyright, 1919
GEORGE H. DORAN COMPANY

HUGH WALPOLE

An Appreciation

JOSEPH HERGESHEIMER

I

IT is with an uncommon feeling of gratification that I am able to begin a paper on Hugh Walpole with the words, in their completest sense, an appreciation. But this rises from no greater fact than a personal difficulty in agreeing with the world at large about the most desirable elements for a novel. Here it is possible to say that Mr. Walpole possesses almost entirely the qualities which seem to me the base, the absolute foundation, of a beauty without which creative writing is empty. In him, to become as specific as possible, there is splendidly joined the consciousness of both the inner and outer worlds.

And, for a particular purpose, I shall put my conviction about his novels into an arbitrary arrangement with no reference to the actual order of appearance of his dignified row of volumes. Such a choice opens with a consideration of what is purely a story

HUGH WALPOLE

of inner pressures, it continues to embrace books devoted principally to the visible world, to London, and ends with a mingling of the seen and unseen in Russia.

Yet, to deny at once all pedantic pretense, it must be made clear that my real concern is with the pleasure, the glow and sense of recognition, to be had from his pages. The evoked emotions, which belong to the heart rather than the head, are the great, the final, mark of the true novelist. And they may be, perhaps, expressed in the single word, magic. Anyone who is susceptible to this quality needs no explanation of its power and importance, while it is almost impossible of description to those upon whom it has no effect. It is quite enough to repeat it . . . magic. At once a train of images, of memories of fine books, will be set in motion. Among them the father of Peter Westcott will appear—a grim evil in a decaying house heavy with the odor of rotten apples; and, accompanying them, the mind will be flooded with the charmed moments of Mr. Walpole's descriptions: Russian nights with frozen stars, rooms swimming placid and strange in old mirrors, golden ballrooms and

HUGH WALPOLE

London dusks, the pale quiver of spring, of vernal fragrance, under the high sooty glass dome of a railroad station.

In this, at once, the remarkable delicacy of his perceptions is made apparent: it is impossible, in thinking of these books, to separate what occurs in the sphere of reality from the vivid pressures, the dim forces, that, lying back of conscious existence, are always gathering like portentous storms behind Mr. Walpole's stories. To have stated so calmly his passionate belief in just these influences was, at the time most of his books were written, an act of that courage he has so persistently extolled. Yet the details of his fortitude belong properly to the examination of individual novels.

Time, however, has altogether justified his spiritual preoccupations: the literature of the surface of things, the sting of onions in a glittering tin bowl, æsthetic boys—still the wistful ghost of Wilde, the flaneur—dragged through the pages of Freud, unlimited sentences in sociology hardly humanized by a tagging of proper names and mechanical desires, have been swept into the dust-bin for temporary reactions and fevers. Nothing can be gained by speculation about the future, it is enough to realize that, in imaginative letters, the school of arrogant materialism has been discredited; and that Mr. Walpole, because of his steadiness in the face of skeptical and mocking devils, has easily, securely, entirely, survived the most blasting and calamitous ordeal men have had yet to meet.

His books, from the first to the last, have not become antiquated; they are as fresh today as they were at any time through the past ten or twelve years; the people in them, true in costume and speech to their various moments, are equally true to that which in man is changeless. They, the novels, are at once provincial, as the best novels invariably are, and universal as any deep penetration of humanity, any considerable artistry, must be. Never merely cosmopolitan, never merely smart—even in his knowledge of smart people—they are sincere without being stupid, serious without a touch of hypocrisy; and on the other hand, light without vapidity, entertaining with never a compromise nor the least descent from the most dignified of engagements.

HUGH WALPOLE

All this, on the plane to which I am confined—the pleasure to be had from accumulated words—is as rare as it is delightful. The world, particularly the world of novel-writing, is choked with solemn pretensions and sly lies; it, the latter, is the fertile field of all the ignorances—the dogmatic, the degenerate, the hysterical, the venal. And, unhappily, there seems to be very nearly a public for each; unhappily the deeply bitten prejudices of men, the secretive hopes of women, control to an amazing degree their opinions of the one medium—the written story—that should be kept superior to all pettiness as a resource solely of alleviation.

Usually great creative writers—gifted, together with pity, with clarity of vision—have dealt in a mood of severity with life; they are largely barred, by their covenant with truth, from the multitude; but Mr. Walpole, not lacking in the final gesture of greatness, has yet the optimism that sees integrity as the master of the terrors. Literature, different from painting and music, serves beauty rather by the detestation of ugliness than in the recording of lyrical felicities. But, again, Mr. Walpole has countless passages of approval, of verbal loveliness, that must make him acceptable not only to a few but to many.

In reading, for example, The Secret City, there is the satisfaction of realizing that the consequent enjoyment rises from an unquestionably pure source. It is a preoccupation to be followed with utter security—for once an admirable thing, a fine thing, is altogether pleasurable.

II

Mr. Walpole's courage in the face of the widest skepticism is nowhere more daring than in The Golden Scarecrow. The book itself, in both conception and composition, presented extraordinary difficulties; one of those themes clear enough in the creative mind, but so deep in implication, so veiled in mystery, so elusive psychologically, that to put it at all upon paper was an accomplishment of very high order. In brief, it is founded on the implication that children born into this faulty world retain, for varying short periods, memories of a serene existence from which they were banished into human consciousness. This remembrance is embodied in the appearance, in dim rooms, against the sunset, in the mists of beginning sensations, of a kindly protecting shape with a beard. The vision is all tenderness and gentle melancholy wisdom . . . Christ!

The particular danger in such a narrative is the almost inescapable shadow of mechanical sentimentality. The conjunction of Christ and little children is perfectly safe to evoke of itself the tear of ready sympathy; and miracles, from the beginning to the late Irish school and later, have been the chosen medium for a useful and easy squeezing of the heart. But, it should be said at once, The Golden Scarecrow is remarkably free from the merely easy, or from cheaply borrowed pathos. It is sustained not only by beautiful phrasing, delicate imagery, but equally by an iron rod of truth. If the vision exists, clad in splendor invisible to anything but innocence, so too does the world Mr. Walpole clearly sees and correctly grasps.

He knows that, while there may be a Saviour for purity in extra-mundane spheres, in London there is no such security: there is always the ugly possibility, no—probability, of accident, of the destruction—by cruelty or envy or vice or sheer carelessness—of youth. In addition to this The Golden Scarecrow gathers importance with the increasing recognition of the extreme importance of the impressions of childhood.

Addressing, with his surprising and justified confidence, the instincts of the newly-born, he follows the human mind opening gradually to the spectacle of living. The progress is established by a succession of episodes, of stories really, bound into a whole by a return, at the book's end, to its beginning statement and mood, and by a single passionate conviction. It is this, certainly, which gives Mr. Walpole his force and beauty—the ability to deliver himself of a high hatred tempered by pity. In The Golden Scarecrow his resentment has for incentive the fatalities brought by chance or design on beings endowed with the finest possibilities.

The arrangement of his novels places this among Studies in Place; and the scene is principally March Square, not far from Hyde Park Corner. There lingers about it the atmosphere of the days of St. Anne, a tranquillity hardly disturbed by the din of

London; and its bricks and greenery, its fountain and statues, one commemorating a general of the Indian Mutiny and the other a mid-Victorian figure, are the last to hold the strains of mendicant street musicians. To these are added the cries of children at their games, garlands of children on the smooth lawn and under the overhanging trees, and, from around the corner, the bells of St. Matthew's.

Each part has for its central figure a child of one of the houses surrounding the Square, from the three-months-old Henry Fitzgeorge, Marquis of Strether, son of the Duchess of Crole, to young John Scarlett, the offspring of a solid K. C., about to leave home for the adventure of public school. But there is, in the range of the book, the greatest possible diversity of children and houses: 'Enery, the simple-witted son of Mrs. Slater, care-taker for Old Lady Cathcart at No. 21; Nancy Ross, daughter of Munty, of potted shrimp fame, in danger of being turned by an impossible mother into an impossible Dresden china figure, but saved by her ugly black little father; Sarah Trefusis, living in a smart

HUGH WALPOLE

little house with green doors and with a widowed mother of the loveliest and most unscrupulous of eyes, Sarah possessed of a sinister devil; Angelina, who would say "Wosy" when she meant Rose, and infuriated her two neat aunts with rather yellow, squashed-looking faces.

It is, perhaps, to Angelina Braid, that the memory most persistently returns; for in the direct story of Angelina and the rag doll she adored above all others—Rachel and Lizzie, two Annies, a Mary, a May, a Blackmoor, a Jap, a Sailor, and a Baby in a Bath—Mr. Walpole has gathered all his art and fury. In it hard meanness, petty destructive tempers, meagreness of heart, are exposed so utterly that it is difficult to suppose anyone, reading it, could ever again support the oppression of a child. The episode of Angelina Braid is told with the utmost restraint, its means are simple, inevitable; but its conveying of irrevocable harm, of the spirit fluttering away from the rigidity of flesh, is matchless.

As a whole The Golden Scarecrow is, considering its heart of mystery, amazingly coherent and satisfactory. From the opening paragraphs, when Hugh Seymour, a lonely imaginative boy, is mentally bullied by a stolid school-master, to the last where, a man, he regains the voice of his Friend, that Friend of before-birth, the book is a living entity. Of the golden scarecrow:

"To their left a dark brown field rose in an ascending wave to a ridge that cut the sky. . . . The field was lit with the soft light of the setting sun. On the ridge of the field something suspended, it seemed, in mid-air, was shining like a golden fire.

" 'What's that,' said Mr. Pidgen again. It's hanging. What the devil!'

"They stopped for a moment, then started across the field. When they had gone a little way Mr. Pidgen paused again.

" 'It's like a man with a gold helmet. He's got legs, he's coming to us.'

"They walked on again. Then Hugh cried, 'Why, it's only an old scarecrow. We might have guessed.'

"The sun, at that instant sank behind the hills and the world was grey."

It was, visibly, but an old scarecrow, with waving tattered sleeves and a tin can that held the light; but it had been, as well, a man in a golden helmet. He had come toward them. That, in a sentence, expresses Mr. Walpole's magic: we see the rags and the tin; and we see, too, the heavenly shining; which is the reality he leaves, as he must, for our determining.

III

In no other novel of Mr. Walpole's are the forces that—perhaps—lie back of life so explicitly expressed as in The Golden Scarecrow, while, of all his books, The Green Mirror is most frankly concerned with terrestrial existence. It is the second in a plan of three called The Rising City, not, he is careful to inform us, a trilogy. Indeed, English society, in the broad sense, placed in London, is the subject of this series; beyond the introduction in The Green Mirror of a few names made familiar by The Duchess of Wrexe, the novels have no actual intercommunication.

They were, however, clearly led up to in other pages, notably Fortitude; but there the dark shapes, like embodied evil passions, were always gathering about the rim of consciousness. But The Green Mirror,

HUGH WALPOLE

except in minor incidences, completely illustrates the spirit in flesh. This it does delightfully with, and this is surprising, a most entertaining humor. Aunt Aggie is one of the old embittered women that Mr. Walpole understands so thoroughly; but, in The Green Mirror, he is more lenient with her than usual. He follows her mind, a mind like the thin scraping jangle of a worn-out music-box, with an amazing flexibility and insight; the latter, in his consideration of Aunt Aggie, predominates. Understanding, of course, dissipates hatred: in the completed picture of ancient maliciousness, positively wicked in intention, the reader is continually cheered by perception of the true, the rare, Comic Spirit.

But she, Aunt Aggie, is comparatively unimportant; the weight of The Green Mirror is the imponderable weight of the Trenchard family. They are not aristocrats, such as the late Duchess of Wrexe, or Roddy Seddon; yet Mr. Walpole makes it clear that, essentially, they are more deeply rooted in tradition, in precedent, than a higher and largely frivolous class.

Here, more than by George Trenchard,

the head of this branch of the family, they are represented by his wife, the mother of Henry and Millicent and, above all else, of Katherine. They are shown in the somber drawing-room of No. 5 Rundle Square, by Westminster in the heart of London, passing and repassing in the aqueous depths of a looking-glass above the mantle:

Mrs. Trenchard, heavy and placid in exterior; the gangling Henry, incurably disorderly and racked by the throes of greensickness; Aunt Aggie and Aunt Betty, sparrow-like, with little glints of cheerfulness; Grandfather Trenchard, as fragile as glass in fastidious silver buckles; and Katherine.

The story itself is the relation of Katherine Trenchard's love for Philip Mark, and how, in the end, it smashed the green mirror of her family. While it is that in detail it is, by implication, the history of the breaking of old English idols. This duality of being, the specific and the symbolical is, certainly, almost the prime necessity for creative literature; and in the published volumes of The Rising City it is everywhere carried out.

HUGH WALPOLE

Philip Mark arrives, through a dense London fog, at the Trenchards' during the celebration of Grandfather Trenchard's birthday—the day, above all, inalterably fixed in their traditions. He is from Russia—Hugh Walpole's land of supreme magic—and his coming is the signal for small irritations, growing complexities, jealousy, that finally set the individual above custom, the present over the past.

Philip Mark, or rather the love of Katherine and Philip, is the cause of so much; but the most impressive, the most important figure in the book, is Katherine's mother. This is a familiar arrangement of Mr. Walpole's; to erect a largely silent negative force, like an evil and sometimes obscene carved god in the shadows, and oppose to it the tragic vivid necessity of youth. In The Green Mirror it takes the shape of maternal jealousy—hard for all its apparent softness of bosom; cruel in spite of undeniable affection, cunning as against an apparent slowness of mentality.

The sweep of the novel is rich with acute observation and borne on by an action rising—as it always must—from causes at once trivial, informal, and inevitable. Philip Mark's past in Moscow, continually coming to the surface by the utmost diversity of means and places; now threatening his happiness, now a foundation for his maturity, furnishes the center of movement, a fact taken up as a weapon or justification by nearly everyone in turn. This, specially to the Trenchards, is of monumental dimensions; but its operation, in Henry's undependable shirt-stud, Aunt Aggie's agitated slap, has the authentic unheroic accent of reality.

The richness of The Green Mirror, however, has its inception in Mr. Walpole's extreme sensitiveness to the spirit of place and hour: all the translations of his action, the changes from place to place, day to night, are recorded with a beautiful and exact care. This is the result of a pictorial sense at once strong and delicate. No one has had more delight from the visible world than Mr. Walpole, and none has been able to capture it better in words:

"In Dean's Yard the snow, with blue evening shadows upon it, caught light from the sheets of stars that tossed and twinkled,

HUGH WALPOLE

stirred and were suddenly immovable. The Christmas bells were ringing; all the lights of the houses in the Yard gathered about her and protected her. What stars there were! What beauty! What silence!"

This conveyance of a crystal mood, without exotic or intricate phrases, without ornament, is the mastery of an art that must be at once brushed with emotion and serene; in it lies the miracle of words, inanimate fragments, brought warmly to life. Katherine, about whom they were written, is sentient as well; a girl stronger in the end than even her mother, a girl who bent being to her will. A lovely girl, concealing behind a completely feminine need, behind clothes never precisely right, Mr. Walpole's beloved courage.

Here particularly, in Katherine Trenchard, the individual and universal humanity are woven one into the other; an immeasurably greater accomplishment than the projecting of mere eccentricity, called, I believe, by the doctors, the creation of character. Anyone, almost, can invent a set of whiskers, a stuttering speech, write imposing indignations into mechanical masks; but only a few have put all youth into a girl of their imagination, on almost no pages do we find the truth that is ourselves.

IV

For Mr. Walpole, however, the dark secret of being was always hidden in the heart of Russia. It has been his land of enchantment, of magic and desire; and it possessed him in the way that Shelley and Browning were Italianate. The English Merchant Marine had the same fascination for Mr. Conrad, the same fascination and incalculable influence. Throughout Hugh Walpole's novels there is the persistent turning to the dream forests and night-ridden cities of Russia, to the mingled simplicity and inexplicable complexity of its men and women.

Russia presented the greatest possible contrast to the England, the English he knew; and, although Mr. Walpole's descriptions of London are steeped in beauty, he has been unable to find there—even in the serenity of March Square—any such creative impulse as Petrograd held for him.

The Russian character, too, with its pe-

HUGH WALPOLE

culiar freedom from the British defects that he specially hated, offered him an uncommonly broad means of expression and intelligibility. Philip Mark's years in Warsaw, his mistress there, Anna, formed an ideal background for the utterly different purity of Katherine Trenchard. So it was inevitable that Mr. Walpole should invade Russia not only with the spirit, but, as well, with the body of his books. This, of course, was brought about by the war, and resulted in the publication of The Dark Forest and The Secret City.

The Dark Forest was, in many ways, a prelude to the latter. Semyonov, the doctor with a square, honey-colored beard, the fatal spirit of the former, accomplishes his final fatality in The Secret City; the narrator of one novel is the narrator of the other; but in The Secret City a great deal that was nebulous—but in no way ineffective—is exactly weighed and expressed.

The surprising quality of The Secret City, and which makes any description of it difficult, is that while it is a tragedy, it is nowhere oppressive. The obvious reason for this is that the story is vividly interesting—

not because it includes a remarkable description of the Russian Revolution, but on account of the humanity and variety of its characters, the depth of emotion and brilliancy of surface. In reality, the Revolution constituted a very serious danger, for in creative fiction, the author, the novel, must be greater than the event. A novel holds within its covers a world of its own, a complete reality which, for the moment, must take the place of all other reality; and the presence in it of an overwhelming contemporary event may well crush the illusion, the shining ball, into dull fragments. But this Mr. Walpole avoids in his concentration upon the essentials of his purpose; the Revolution, as a fact, fades before the more enduring veracity, and importance, of his imagination.

Vera and Nina, the fretted Markovitch, and Jerry Lawrence, tied in a knot of passion and longing and bitterness, now struggling blindly and now illuminated with devastating flashes of realization, are more compelling than the accidents of wars and shifting governments. They are the human means of the drama, but—again—it is a pressure lying back of living that is mainly

HUGH WALPOLE

important. In The Secret City, Petrograd itself controls the mood of the action. Mr. Walpole has seen it in a unity of tone far more perfect than his grasp of London. He sees it impressively somber, an iron city mostly in the grip of winter, its blackness emphasized by glittering, immaculate snow, remote and thinly pure skies, and the crystal stars to which he is so individually sensitive. It is, in The Secret City, an evil place, with bare, wind-swept files of apartment houses, broad avenues emptied by the staccato rattle of machine guns and suffocating slums with dead canals stirred with the vision of slow-rising, scaly monsters.

Against this, however, there are glimpses of a peasant, a symbolical reality, deeply bearded and grave and patient, standing, it might be, on a bridge or disappearing into the dark. Yet there are no prophecies, no auguries of a future regenerated from without. Mr. Walpole is not concerned with the temporary plasters, the nostrums, of propaganda. He rests serene in the novelist's isolation from small responsibilities, addressed only to the qualities at the base of humanity from which current fevers rise.

HUGH WALPOLE

And here, at last, he has combined the inner and outer pressures of which I spoke at the beginning. While it is true that Petrograd strikes the persistent keynote of The Secret City, while he sees monsters stirring and records dreams woven into the texture of actuality, these are projections of the deep significance of Lawrence and Markovitch; signs and visions are unnecessary with their complete expression of the states of the spirit. Lawrence, the Englishman, slow, fixed in honor and duty, romantically pure, and the Russian, worn by doubt, forever lost in the waste between performance and idea, oppose, perhaps, in little, their countries. Certainly they illustrate Mr. Walpole's own questioning and offer facts, entirely convincing, for the support of his intricate structures.

Semyonov, who, under almost any other hand, would have degenerated into a mere villain, is presented with Mr. Walpole's passion for entire understanding, that comprehension which banishes contempt. Vastly intricate, a character seen on a hundred sides, he still remains intelligible, consistent; a consistency which permits him to take naturally his place in a story at once involved and simple. He is, above everything, a spoiled soul; the unhappiest possible example of the oil of heaven arbitrarily imposed on the water of earth. His is the agony of the animal confronted with the mysteries of the spirit; and the ruin which emanates from his torment and skeptical detachment is the result as much of his superiority as of his fault.

It is, more than anything else, the fusion in The Secret City that, at the time of its publication, made it the most notable of Mr. Walpole's novels. As a story it is enthralling, the mere progress of the action is irresistible; the atmosphere, the envelopment of color, is without a rent, a somber veil like a heavy mist subduing the flashes of red at the horizon, muffling the sounds and glints of passion, absorbing the shouted ambitions of men. That it is not Russia, but himself, Mr. Walpole has been very careful to point out; it is simply the land of magic to which he has been always drawn, and which, conceivably, having explored, he'll leave, returning to England.

HUGH WALPOLE
V

As a whole, Hugh Walpole's novels maintain an impressive unity of expression; they are the distinguished presentation of a distinguished mind. Singly, and in a group, they hold possibilities of infinite development. This, it seems to me, is most clearly marked in their superiority to the cheap materialism that has been the insistent note of the prevailing optimistic fiction. There is a great deal of happiness in Mr. Walpole's pages, but it isn't founded on surface vulgarities of appetite; the drama of his books is not sapped by the automatic security of invulnerable heroics. Accidents happen, tragic and humorous, the life of his novels is checked in black and white, often shrouded in grey. The sun moves and stars come out; youth grows old; charm fades; girls may or may not be pretty; his old women—

But there he is inimitable, the old gentlewomen, or caretakers, dry and twisted, brittle and sharp, the repositories of emotion—vanities and malice and self-seeking—like echoes of the past, or fat and loquacious with alcoholic sentimentality, are wonderfully

HUGH WALPOLE

ingratiating. They gather like shadows, ghosts, about the feet of the young, and provide Mr. Walpole with one of his main resources—the restless turning away of the young from the conventions, the prejudices and inhibitions, of yesterday. He is singularly intent upon the injustice of locking age about the wrists of youth; and, with him, youth is very apt to escape, to defy authority set in years . . . only to become, in time, age itself.

This, of course, is inescapable: the old are the old, and not least among their infirmities is the deadening of their sensibilities, the hardening of their perceptions. But then, as well, the young are the young, and youth is folly, blind revolt, contumacy. Here is perpetual drama and, with it, Mr. Walpole's hatred of brutality is drawn into practically all his pictures of childhood, as, for example, the school in Fortitude.

In all this he recognizes clearly that beauty and ugliness are twisted into the fibre of man, they are man; without one the other must cease—in spite of the contrary legend—to exist. Beauty lies in struggle, in the overcoming of evil; without struggle there is not only no story, there is no fineness; and without evil there can be no good. Victory, certainly, is not unheard of; but it is rare, the result of amazing courage, strength, or amazing luck. To say that anyone, almost, can triumph over life, that temptation is easily cast aside, the devil denied on every hand, is one of the most insidious lies imaginable. It is an error into which Hugh Walpole has never fallen; the progress of his books has been an increasing recognition of the tragic difficulty of any accomplishment whatever; and, as time goes by, such success becomes smaller, more momentary, and more heroic.

The course of the novelist is from the bright surface of life inward to its impenetrable heart, from the striking the easy, the lovely, to the hopelessly hidden mystery of being; and Mr. Walpole is steadily, perhaps unconsciously, entering the profounder darkness. It is a march practically condemned to failure at the start; but, not only unavoidable, it is the only attempt worth consideration. Not a happy fate, God knows, to leave everything that the world, that people, most applaud; there is no possibility of mistake about the latter—the beauty that is truth is not popular in a society which, blind to its transitory and feeble condition, must see itself as the rulers of creation.

Yet this, for its part, is entirely commendable, the illusion necessary to the sustaining of an affair difficult at best. Novels that ring a musical chime of bells, an anodyne for the heart, are always sure of their welcome; they represent an appreciation in the dimension of width; while the reception of The Secret City goes rather in the direction of depth. At the same time there is that strange absence of oppression already noted, a story always enjoyable for its suspense, the play of character on character.

The result of the commingling, in Hugh Walpole, of the seen and the unseen! If he were a conventional materialist the disasters to the flesh would be unrelieved tragedy, his Roderick Seddon, paralyzed for life, would be, to the haphazard mind, unsupportable; but Mr. Walpole manages to put the emphasis on Seddon's spirit, that proves to be above accident. When Markovitch, at the end of his unendurable suffering, kills Semyonov, there is no horror, but only pity.

HUGH WALPOLE

The novel, of course, is the man; and the emotions of The Secret City are the emotions of Mr. Walpole; it is merely the extension, by an art and a record, of the mind of its creator. The pity of the reader is Mr. Walpole's; wherever his novel goes, wherever it is read, if there is any response it is one touched with dignity and wisdom. There is the validity of the superior accomplishment, the payment for the failure implied in the greater undertaking: the recognition of the insignificant novel is insignificant, it is a part of the life flashing for a moment in the sunlight, dead, forgotten, by evening. But if there is any discoverable solidarity in men, any hope of final escape from intolerable futility, it must be assisted, if ever so little, by the simple honesty, the communication of fortitude, in books founded, at least, on what is changeless, inevitable, to living.

When these qualities form the pleasure of the multitude, as they now do of a minority, the world will be a vastly different and better place. Yet this is not primarily, not at all, I personally feel, Mr. Walpole's concern: he is the carver on the stone, the embellisher on parchment; his art is the sign, the recompense, of civilization. He is the pot of geraniums in the window, the beauty, utility, above utility. Not for nothing do we allow the philosophies, the doctrines, even the humanities, of the past to fall into oblivion, while we preserve any marble fragment of beauty we are so fortunate as to recover.

Mr. Walpole is a part of that great necessity, of the longing, really, for perfection, for perfect beauty. This, too, is the only salvation for ease; the animal, when he is replete, fat, dies; and man, successful in the flesh, degenerates. There only spirit, beauty, animates the clay. Roses, in the end, are more important than cabbages. Here, Hugh Walpole, cultivating the fine flowers of his imagination, setting out his gardens in the waste, is indispensable . . . very few have accomplished that.

NOVELS *by* HUGH WALPOLE

Description and Comment

THE SECRET CITY

WHAT is the secret city of the title? Petrograd? Yes, partly. But much more is it the citadel of the Russian proverb which recites: "In each man's heart there is a secret town at whose altars the true prayers are offered!" And so what we have in this book before us is first (and always foremost) the story of several lives. Petrograd itself, with its insane atmosphere on the eve of the Revolution, is painted for us persistently, with many patient and wonderful brush strokes. The Revolution, or the first weeks of it, are narrated for us with an eyewitness's veracity and an eyewitness's incompleteness. But Petrograd and the Revolution . . . all that . . . are put before us only so far as they enter into the lives of a few people—a family of Russians and three casual Englishmen. Which is as it should be. Petrograds change, revolutions come and go; but the secret city of the human heart is not transformed. Human motives remain. Human passions ebb and flow. Human hopes perish—and are reborn.

The people of Mr. Walpole's novel are completely realized. They are as much alive as if they moved in the flesh before you. The reader may be baffled by them—many a reader will be, though to most readers they will be comprehensible before the closing chapters. But baffling or not, there is no disbelieving in them. Two of the most important—Alexei Petrovitch Semyonov and John Durward, the narrator—are characters in Mr. Walpole's earlier novel, *The Dark Forest*. It is not absolutely necessary that before reading *The Secret City* you should read *The Dark Forest,* but it is much to be desired that you do so. Otherwise you will be unable to fathom Alexei Petrovitch (the overshadowing character) as adequately as you ought to from his first entrance.

But about the others, the others besides the sinister Alexei Petrovitch. Take poor old Markovitch, for example. It's not easy, of course, to see him as anything but a self-befooled, ridiculous figure until you grasp that he had three ideals to live up to. The first was his wife, Vera; then there were his hopeless inventions; lastly, there was Russia. Came a time when, as young Bohun, one of the Englishmen, put it: "He'd lost Russia, he was losing Vera, and he wasn't very sure about his inventions." At the last he clung to Russia, hopefully. This revolution meant something wonderful for her—and for the whole world!

Take Vera, beautiful and with immortal pride; with a great and candid courage, too. She had

HUGH WALPOLE

her sister, the girlish Nina, she had her husband. What was this tragedy of love that came to her and destroyed everything? Nina, tempestuous, lovable, like a child—why in the name of all that is merciful should *she* have to suffer? Thank God! there was a happy ending here!

Others—a half dozen or so—that we mustn't speak of singly. Even such minor characters as Uncle Ivan and Baron Wilderling are etched perfectly. We would say a few words about the background.

Mr. Walpole makes Petrograd as memorable a city as does Tolstoy his Moscow, with Napoleon gazing upon its rounded domes. And that is memorable indeed, as any one who ever read *War and Peace* will certify. An intensely colorful city, lighted by stars and bonfires, exhaling the stink of the swamp and Rasputin's corpse, coldly menaced by the frozen Neva River, a volcano of human destiny with its thick ice melting rapidly from the heat of terrible flames underneath. A city where a great slimy beast seems to appear apocalyptically from the sheeted waters of the canal. A city where always there stands silhouetted against the evening glow the immense figure of a black-bearded peasant, grave, controlled, thoughtful, watching. A city of dream—only the dream is true.

There can be no doubt about it; this is a noteworthy book, a beautifully written book and—what

HUGH WALPOLE

is best of all—a book with a backbone. You may like it or you may not; you will be unable, we believe, to withhold admiration.—From a review in *The New York Sun*.

"Hugh Walpole has proved his right to eminence. *The Secret City* is a worthy successor to *The Dark Forest*. His art in presentation is consummate. But the trait that stands out in his writings is his humanity."—*Chicago Daily News*.

"This is, we believe, Mr. Walpole's best novel, a finer book even than *The Dark Forest*. Its descriptive passages are many of them superb; we get the sense of the strange and alien forces lying beneath the somewhat Europeanized surface of Petrograd in a truly remarkable way."—*New York Times*.

"It is one of Mr. Walpole's achievements in this book that along with his philosophic study of Russian minds and matters, he maintains a running, throbbing story of the romance-tragedy of the Markovitch home. Its form and style confirm it in a place of great literary distinction. Being the sort of book one desires to keep as well as to read, it sustains the final test of a fictional work."—*New York World*.

"Hugh Walpole has equalled himself at his best and far surpassed himself at his second best. A novel of the rare sort that is meant for the delight of discriminating readers."—*Washington Star*.

HUGH WALPOLE

"The best recommendation of his novel is its excellent quality as a story: its absorbing interest in character."—*Boston Herald*.

"The story is tensely dramatic in its incidents and situations, its characters are real and interesting. . . . You cannot merely read this book, for if you mean to keep on you must think and keep on thinking."—*San Francisco Chronicle*.

"Mr. Walpole is a story-teller with something in him besides fine facility, and it is fascinating to consider this excellent example of his work."—*The New Republic*.

"Somehow, by the magic of his words, Mr. Walpole, in his portrayal of a people in the process of evolving, makes his readers understand better what has taken place in Russia than political experts in many an analytical treatise."—*Springfield Union*.

"One of the best sustained, most continuously interesting and dramatic stories Mr. Walpole has written."—*New York Globe*.

"It is his best work as a piece of literature and it is his most important as an ethical, sociological and political study."—*New York Tribune*.

JEREMY

THE real beauty, tenderness and gaiety of childhood is an elusive thing—too elusive often to be caught and pressed into words. By some magic of his own Hugh Walpole has made live

HUGH WALPOLE

again in *Jeremy* the childhood that we all knew and that we turn back to with infinite longing.

With affectionate humorousness, Mr. Walpole tells the story of Jeremy and his two sisters, Helen and Mary Cole, who grow up in Polchester, a quiet English Cathedral town. There is the Jampot, who is the nurse; Hamlet, the stray dog; Uncle Samuel, who paints pictures and is altogether "queer"; of course, Mr. and Mrs. Cole, and Aunt Amy.

Mr. Walpole has given his narrative a rare double appeal, for it not only recreates for the adult the illusion of his own happiest youth, but it unfolds for the child-reader a genuine and moving experience with real people and pleasant things. No child will fail to love the birthday in the Cole household, the joyous departure for the sea and the country in the long vacation.

"A story of the most human elements, tender, witty, penetrating in a breath. It is the study of one year in a boy's life. . . . Mr. Walpole goes straight to the heart of the child for his inspiration, and never strays outside the narrow limits of a child's experience. It is 'the real thing,' wonderfully remembered, and most sympathetically and unaffectedly recorded."—*Daily Telegraph*.

HUGH WALPOLE
THE DARK FOREST

OUT of Russia, where Hugh Walpole had been serving with the Russian Red Cross, came this strange, wonderful, exotic book, containing an inexplicable treasure of beauty,—the glamour of the Russian forest, the scent of blossoming orchards, the wistful heroism of young Russian soldiers. *The Dark Forest* would be an astonishing performance if only in this—that Walpole has conceived and written a *Russian novel in English*. But there are scenes that are the most vividly realized moments of which Walpole has ever written. Scenes which the *Westminster Gazette* calls "the equal of the most dramatic passages in English fiction." Mystical, poetical, spiritual, the theme of *The Dark Forest* is the triumph of the soul over death. One may read in it an allegory of the soul of Russia.

"To say that this book is remarkable is only to lay hold on a convenient word as expressive of at least a part of the sensation the story produces. Here is a book for which many of us have dimly waited; a book that transcends the outer facts and reveals the inner significance of war. *The Dark Forest* is a love story of unusual beauty, as well as a story of war. Who, having read it, will forget this book; at once awful and beautiful? It must be read, for neither quotation nor description is capable of giving more than a bare hint of the

HUGH WALPOLE

nobleness, the intensity of this work of art so deeply rooted in reality."—*New York Times*.

"Of all the novels that have come out of European battlefields there is probably none of such scope, such penetrating analysis and such completely spiritual quality as Hugh Walpole's *Dark Forest*. It is many novels in one. . . . It is instinct with the sense of spiritual adventure. It is young, finely emotional, stamped with the consciousness of beauty and infinity, of heroism and horror, love of life and the vision of death."—*Eleanore Kellogg, in The Chicago Evening Post*.

"At last there issues a novel with qualities of greatness and the promise of endurance. Hugh Walpole's *Dark Forest* should, indeed, as a work of literary art, easily survive the terror and the turmoil."—*New York World*.

"Dostoievsky compressed within a few pages. A remarkable book indeed—beyond doubt the most notable novel inspired by the war."—*New York Tribune*.

"*The Dark Forest* is the first fine story product of a high order of creative art we have had from the European war."—*Boston Herald*.

"The very spirit of Russia is here. This is unusual. Walpole appears to have become gifted in a few months with the true Russian literary method. Its magic is his."—*Boston Transcript*.

"It is a story of sustained power; tragic import

HUGH WALPOLE

and impress, and careless disregard of western conventions. The rapt mysticism and unselfish devotion of the heroine; the downright, uncompromising materialism of her Russian lovers; the pathetic appeal of Trenchard's loyalty, and the situation finally developed by the heroine's untimely taking off—these, in connection with the continually recurring episodes of grim war, afford large opportunity for originality of treatment and characteristic, forceful dramatism." — *Philadelphia North Amercian*.

"Such a novel needed the war for its background. It needed the war for its origin. It could only have been planned on the battle line. It could be written for and appreciated by only such an audience as has been prepared by the melancholy of catastrophe. War's blood is in it, war's nerves and sinews. It is the very soul, upheaved, bereft, of war. It is the one great romance that has come from a world of armies."—*New York Evening Sun*.

"*The Dark Forest* is a novel of extraordinary beauty and power. . . . It is a work of art, unqualifiedly a great book."—*Review of Reviews*.

"Hugh Walpole's *The Dark Forest* is the best story yet written about the war that we have read." —*New York Globe*.

HUGH WALPOLE
THE GREEN MIRROR

THE title of *The Green Mirror* is symbolic. In the drawing-room of the London house of the Trenchards, not far from Westminster Abbey, it represented the past and the present of a great and typical English family.

"Above the wide stone fireplace was a large old gold mirror, a mirror that took into its expanse the whole of the room, so that, standing before it, with your back to the door, you could see everything that happened behind you. The mirror was old, and gave to the view that it embraced some comfortable touch, so that everything within it was soft and still and at rest." Henry Trenchard, gazing into it, saw "the reflection of the room, the green walls, the green carpet, the old faded green place, like moss covering dead ground. Soft, dark, damp. . . . The people, his family, his many, many relations, his world, he thought, were all inside the mirror—all imbedded in that green, soft, silent inclosure. He saw, stretching from one end of England to the other, in all provincial towns, in neat little houses with neat little gardens, in cathedral cities with their sequestered closes, in villages with the deep green lanes leading up to the rectory gardens, in old country places by the sea, all these people happily, peacefully sunk up to their very necks in the green moss. . . . His own family passed before him. His grandfather, his great-aunt Sarah,

HUGH WALPOLE

his mother and his father, Aunt Aggie and Aunt Betty, Uncle Tim, Millicent, Katherine."

Katherine embodied the spirit of revolt from the tyranny of family. When Philip Mark, a young Englishman, who has spent the greater part of his life in Russia, and whose experiences have made him more Russian than English, comes wooing in tempestuous fashion, she throws off the yoke of her family and chooses for herself. It is when the ties of family are about to be shattered that Henry Trenchard, in a fit of passion, flings a book at Mark, the invader, who has shaken Katherine's faith in the family, and, instead of hitting Mark, demolishes the mirror. "There was a tinkle of falling glass, and instantly the whole room seemed to tumble into pieces, the old walls, the old prints and water colors, the green carpet, the solemn bookcases, the large armchairs—and with the room the house, Westminster, Garth, Glebeshire, Trenchard and Trenchard traditions—all represented now by splinters and fragments of glass."

"*The Green Mirror,* the second in the series of the *Rising City* series, which was opened by *The Duchess of Wrexe,* is not only quite individual in style but the story is told with a most vivid sense of that which the realists are supposed to lack— form. But there is no sacrifice of truth to it. The psychology of the characters rings true. The reaction of an unimaginative, sober, righteous family to a prospective son-in-law has seldom been better done. The story will add to Mr. Walpole's reputation and will not at all suffer from the fact that it was written before the war, as his overmodest preface might indicate that he fears."—*Chicago Evening Post*.

"Henry James once said of the author that he was 'saturated' with youth, and in this story Walpole idealizes the triumph of the youth of the new generation that breaks the cords that bind it to the old and starts out for itself—a careful, coherent and brilliant study."—*St. Louis Globe-Democrat*.

"This is a splendid study, the love story is charming and altogether the book is an exceptionally good piece of work."—*The New York Tribune*.

"In *The Green Mirror* Hugh Walpole shows his masterly skill in building up a really dramatic novel out of plot material that is almost without action. His crises are always crises of feeling and no one equals Mr. Walpole in his analysis of the feeling of his characters and his exposition of their motives, development and change."—*Cincinnati Enquirer*.

"*The Green Mirror* will serve further to intensify the belief that Mr. Walpole is one of the great novelists of the time. The reviewer does not hesitate to proclaim the conviction that he will be the greatest novelist of his generation who uses English as the medium of his expression."—*Providence Journal*.

HUGH WALPOLE

"Mr. Walpole has written a most unusual story and has handled it in an exceedingly capable manner. His plot is so out of the ordinary and is so well worked out that *The Green Mirror* may well be classed as an exceptional novel and as such is likely to rank high among the fiction of the present years."—*Brooklyn Daily Eagle*.

"As a picture of contemporary life, the novel contains some elements that are as fundamental as those which make Dickens characters of old London real flesh and blood to readers of today. As a study in motives animating society the book is worthy the best traditions of English literature. *The Green Mirror* is a distinct contribution to literature."—*Detroit News Tribune*.

"*The Green Mirror* has not one touch of aniline in all its warm colors, rich presences and faithful portraiture. It is a fine novel, grappling bravely with the great ironies of mother-love."—*New Republic*.

"In the development and disclosure of the essential and incidental scenes of the domestic embroilment following upon disclosure of the central situation Walpole vindicates his title to the primacy in the ranks of British fictionists who have undertaken to represent imaginatively the source, spirit and outcome of insularity translated in terms of selfishness and family pride. It is life transcribed as inexorable and fatalistic as *Fortitude* and *Duchess of Wrexe*."—*Philadelphia North American*.

HUGH WALPOLE
FORTITUDE

THE novel which first introduced Walpole to America was *Fortitude,* that most beautiful, most strong story of a man's fight against heredity and circumstance for mastery over himself. The theme of the book lies in a saying of the Cornish fisherman, old Frosted Moses: " 'Tisn't life that matters, but the courage you bring to it."

Peter Westcott, son of the black and sullen generations of Scaw House, heard Frosted Moses say that, as he, a tiny little boy, crouched in a chimney corner at the old inn and heard the sages talk of ancient Cornish legends, and of the glory of the great world without. So did he imbibe a spirit of adventure which he never lost.

He left Scaw House and his gloomy father, fought his way through school, through the welter of a London boarding-house, through poverty and failure to success as a novelist. But his struggle and his success were not the poor desire for petty fame which many conventional heroes of fiction regard as struggle. What he desired in life was fortitude, not headlines; the power to face failure as well as the ability to become known. The spirit of adventure, humanity, these ever stirred him, and he lost neither in becoming a victor.

Of the woman who loved Peter and the woman whom Peter loved, Walpole makes a magnificent

HUGH WALPOLE

love story. There were many hours of dramatic misunderstanding in the passion that sprang up between the solid, broad-shouldered Peter, with his quiet desire to write and be friendly toward all sorts of people, and Clare, the slender, nervous, gay, red-haired girl who had always been protected. But there was a great and beautiful wonder of passion as well; and the happiness of the little London house to which they returned from the honeymoon is not to be forgotten.

And throughout there are very many people who are not to be forgotten—Stephen, the Cornishman, huge and bearded and bewildered and inarticulate, loving the youngster Peter and the girl he could not have, tramping the hard white roads of England, an outcast for love; Zanti, the "foreigner," always a-quiver with babbling excitement over some new adventure on whose trail he was following; quiet Norah, untidy and pale, yet burning with a love which gave back his fortitude to Peter when it seemed lost; Cardillac, the elegant; Galleon, the great novelist; the kiddies who adored big Peter; Peter's own son, whom he so terribly loved.

It is a marvellous gallery, and more marvellous, even, is the gallery of scenes, not painted in long and laborious descriptions, but in quick snatches, which show the fact that Walpole watches sky and wind and tree as does no other novelist.

Do you not come from the heart of dusty coun-

HUGH WALPOLE

try back to the sea again as you read this? If you do not, then you do not love the sea, whose very breath is here in this description from *Fortitude:*

"They were at the top of the hill now. The sea broke upon them with an instant menacing roar. Between them and this violence there was now only moorland, rough with gorse bushes, uneven with little pits of sand, scented with sea pinks, with stony tracks here and there where the moonlight touched it."

Put this with the first lines in *Maradick at Forty* and you have a whole seaside holiday:

"The gray twilight gives to the long, pale stretches of sand the sense of something strangely unreal. As far as the eye can reach, it curves out into the mist, the last vanishing garments of some fleeing ghost. The sea comes smoothly, quite silently, over the breast of it; there is a trembling whisper as it catches the highest stretch of sand and drags it for a moment down the slope; then, with a little sigh, creeps back again a defeated lover."

Or, if you will have the soul of the gay city, here it is in a quotation from *Fortitude:*

"The street stirred with the pattering of dogs out for an airing. The light slid down the sky— voices rang in the clear air softly as though the dying day besought them to be tender. The colours of the shops, of the green trees, of slim and beautifully dressed houses, were powdered with

HUGH WALPOLE

gold-dust; the church in Sloane Square began to ring its bells."

But it is not so much beautiful imagery, not so much interesting people, that distinguish *Fortitude* and make it a great-hearted book, as the courage for life, the demand for fortitude.

"*Fortitude* is a book in which the writer has put much passionate intensity of thought and conviction. It has no faults of insincerity, weakness, nor poverty of mind or heart. It is fascinating. It is the expression of a born writer. One reads it all. There is humor, there is generosity; as of some big man overflowing with ideas. There is a noble spirit in the book that blows fresh upon one, like a wind from the sea. The wind may have blown through desperate places and seen bitter things, but it is clean and bracing, and one is glad of it."—*Hildegarde Hawthorne in The New York Times*.

"*Fortitude* is a story that one will like to linger over after it is read. It is reminiscent of Thackeray at his best, mellowed with the charity of well-proportioned truth."—*New York American*.

"*Fortitude* is impressive. Its revelations of life strike deeply into those springs of youth from which are filled the wells of manhood."—*The New York World*.

"This novel is a genuine performance. All is worked out in the finest detail, like the careful etching of a great, stone-made cathedral."—*The Chicago Evening Post.*

"Hugh Walpole is a literary force to be reckoned with. He knows life; he is not afraid to depict it. He can be sympathetic without being sentimental. He is afraid neither of pleasure nor pain —nor of seeming to fear the conventionalities. He has the true idea of romance. He knows that the enchanted land of adventure may be found in a London boarding house as surely as on stormy seas or in deep hidden gold mines. He knows that man's fiercest battles seldom are fought to the accompaniment of cannon. He knows that loneliness is one of the hardest, one of the most universal of humanity's tests and sorrows. *Fortitude* is a book to read more than once, to ponder. Instinct with life and vigor, lovers of sentiment, fighting, psychology, romance, realism, each will find it worth while."—*The Chicago Record-Herald.*

"*Fortitude* is a book of splendid strength and significance. It is done with much care for workmanship and with a large understanding of the meaning of life, so proving doubly worth while. . . . Throughout the book is marked by a penetrating knowledge of humanity, so that it brings one continually into touch with real people and real human crises."—*The Continent.*

"Mr. Hugh Walpole has the faculty of infusing vibrant life into his characters in fiction, and in

HUGH WALPOLE

Fortitude he presents one of the strongest and best novels of the season."—*The Baltimore Sun*.

"The people here are as real as life. The theme is big. The movement is controlled and steady, a leisurely movement, as stories that deal with character rather than action must be. The sketches of London, in their whimsically personal note, make one think of Dickens in the same field. The whole is big in every sense. One of the two or three or maybe four novels of the year that will live to celebrate even a single birthday."—*The Washington Evening Star*.

"There is not a dull page in the book. Its people are real flesh and blood beings, with courage, with love and with humor in their souls. All of them are interesting, while the circumstances which surround them in *Fortitude* increase the delight of the many readers the book is certain to achieve."—*The Boston Globe*.

"The book is full of thought. Mr. Walpole has written a chapter of life, pure and simple. The reader cannot skip one page."—*The Philadelphia Public Ledger*.

"*Fortitude* is a great book. It marks the arrival of Hugh Walpole as a novelist to be reckoned with. We will await further performance with an anticipation like that with which we look forward to a new Five Towns tale by Bennett."—*Norma Bright Carson in Book News Monthly*.

HUGH WALPOLE

"One of the remarkable novels of the year. This is a great book."—*The San Francisco Chronicle*.

"This book of humor, romance, and realism is a pæan of youth and strength and love, a valiant and bracing sermon."—*The Nashville Tennessean*.

THE DUCHESS OF WREXE

WALPOLE'S constantly increasing perception of the breadth and dignity of the world has given to *The Duchess of Wrexe: A Romantic Commentary* a spaciousness, a universality which make it apply to the big problems of today wherever found—yet his ceaseless interest in human nature keep it a pleasant tale to read, with a surge of power.

It is the story of the second generation's struggle for freedom, for the right to think and grow and love and form social circles as it wills, against the tradition which commends them to do as tradition wills. It is the struggle which is identical all over the world, whether in London or San Francisco, Paris or Peking. It is the struggle which expresses itself in feminism, in changing art, in growing rationalism of manner and speech and thought.

The Duchess of Wrexe is the autocrat of the autocrats; the modern cavalier; old, shriveled, feeble of body, but keen of eye as ever, with her cynical wit and sophisticated manner unchanged, who until she is dead will never give up her fight to keep the

HUGH WALPOLE

race of cavaliers ruling the nation, to keep the despised race of ordinary people (especially the *nouveau riche*) in their places. From her darkened rooms, where she sits in a great chair with grim china dragons on either side, she plots against the spread of democracy shrewdly, ruthlessly, ceaselessly.

The spirit of the times is proving too much for the Duchess. But she fights on. However glad the reader may be of the defeat of all the tyranny for which the Duchess stands, he cannot but be touched by her plucky fight and the grim persistence of her cynical wit.

It may be mentioned that Walpole does not, like many writers, draw on imagination entirely for his pictures of aristocracy and smart society. Essential democrat though he is, Hugh Walpole is the cousin of the Earl of Orford, the son of a bishop, and a descendant of the famous prime minister, Sir Robert Walpole.

"*The Duchess of Wrexe* is a wonderful piece of creative character study. There is a maturity, a sureness of touch in the book that marks the man who knows just what he can do with his medium and does it enthusiastically and well."—*Book News Monthly*.

"A definite and notable addition to English letters is made when a new novel by Hugh Walpole

HUGH WALPOLE

is published. His latest book, *The Duchess of Wrexe,* deals on large elemental lines with the restless, changing spirit of the time. To the strange medley of modern life the novelist's powers of invention, description and characterization are highly addressed. His spirited and finished portrayal of one phase of the changing social order exemplifies finely and naturally the picturesque realism of new-century romance."—*Philadelphia North American.*

"*The Duchess of Wrexe* stimulates thought and encourages reflection. It contains a multitude of ideas and it also allows the reader to think for himself. It is energetic and vigorous without being truculent; it sets forth social conditions without being polemic. It is genuinely a story, and it is at the same time a suggestive commentary on life. *On every page it dignifies the art of the novelist.* . . . With all his subtlety, with all his restraint, with all his ingenuity in making it a social study, Mr. Walpole has not made *The Duchess of Wrexe* any the less effective as a story. It is a novel that entertains, that charms. On a single page of it will be found more about mankind and life than is discoverable in the entirety of many another novel. . . . He has lavished upon it ideas, situations, events and characters sufficient for the lifework of numerous other novelists."—*Boston Transcript.*

"Those who take Mr. Walpole's work as a plain story will find it of compelling interest. Those

HUGH WALPOLE

who read its message complete will be impressed by the sense of a great theme thoughtfully and powerfully presented. There is no flattery in the statement that this book is *one of the really great pieces of modern fiction.*"—*New York World*.

"All the grim, unyielding pride of race of England's old autocracy is made incarnate in the personality of one aged woman, the ever-dominating title-character in this admirable study of changing social orders. It is a heroic picture that the author paints of this grim old head of the house of Beaminster. She stands out supreme amid the pages, one of the most notable figures put into a book in a long time."—*Philadelphia Press*.

"Walpole has strengthened his claim to position by proving that he is not a man of one book, for *The Duchess of Wrexe* is without doubt one of the big novels of the year. It is a novel of extreme significance."—*Samuel Abbott in The Boston Post*.

THE GOLDEN SCARECROW

"IF you love enough we are with you everywhere —forever"—that is the word of the little children that stupid people call "dead." Always here, playing in the room they loved. Such is the end of *The Golden Scarecrow,* the most original book by the author of *Fortitude*. It is the story of a dozen children living about a spacious old square,

HUGH WALPOLE

a square filled with leisure and the sound of leaves, in the heart of London. The son of a duke is one, and one the forlornly playing child of a housekeeper who drank and was untidy, but their lives were all bound together by the Friend—who is the Friend of Stevenson's child-verses—who in dangerous or unhappy moments comes to children and with his great warm arm guides them. . . . There is a wonderful fancifulness in *The Golden Scarecrow*, a mellow and gentle beauty; and a really remarkable ability to enter into the children's own world, where carpets are vast moors, and the fire whispers secrets, and the lashing out of a whip of wind suggests things vast and secret and perilous. Mr. Walpole has "loved enough"; has so loved children and the little land of the imagination that he has put into this book the quality which can never be quite plumbed—tenderness. And it is not the awkward tenderness of the person not born to write; but graceful and perfect and winning as a Greek vase.

"The fact that childhood is not a mere prelude to adult life but worth while for its own sake has seldom been more beautifully expressed."—*Chicago Evening Post*.

"Few adults preserve their line of communication with that world of fancy so real to children. But when one of rare fancy visualizes it a chord of kinship is struck; memory rolls back the years, and

HUGH WALPOLE

the heart responds. Barrie did it in *The Little White Bird*. Hugh Walpole joins him with *The Golden Scarecrow*."—*Boston Herald*.

"Only those readers of Mr. Walpole's novels who have missed any real sense of them will be surprised by this singularly attractive series of sketches. There is an infinite pathos and a quite exquisite charm in the first sketch, the one which suggests the spirit of them all. . . . It cannot be too strongly insisted upon that in these child-studies there is not a whiff of the psuedo-sentiment about childhood which in some writings has reached the nauseating point. Mr. Walpole simply has the very rare gift of actually getting the child's point of view, and we always feel that he really understands what he is talking about."—*Providence Journal*.

"In one sense it bears kinship to Barrie's *Peter Pan* and Maeterlink's *Blue Bird,* for although it is unlike either of these fairy tales in material and treatment, it is related to them in that it recreates for older readers the magical world of the imagination that plays so large a part in the lives of little folk. Mr. Walpole writes with charm and tenderness."—*Philadelphia Press*.

"It is as beautiful as it is unusual—a wonderfully sympathetic and illuminating study of the mind of the child done with an understanding and sympathy so complete that it is uncanny."—*New York Evening Mail*.

HUGH WALPOLE
THE WOODEN HORSE

WITH hesitation one approaches the first novel of an author whose growth has been so steady as that of Walpole. It is therefore a double delight to find *The Wooden Horse* a thoroughly good story. Indeed, it has in it certain qualities which should, as Walpole's work becomes more and more known in mass, be one of his most popular. For it is filled with the youth's first joy of expression; its excitement about life and its yearning for strange new roads.

The Wooden Horse is the story of the Trojans, a family which accepted as tranquilly as did the Duchess of Wrexe the belief that they were the people for whom the world was created. But when Harry Trojan came home after twenty years in New Zealand, with the democracy learned by working his hands, he was the "wooden horse" who boldly carried into the Trojan walls a whole army of alien ideals, which made of that egotistic family a group of human beings content to be human.

Interesting are his struggles against stubborn prejudice; dreamlike the pictures of the old Trojan house, rising from the edge of the gray Cornish cliff like an older cliff, yet surrounded by fragrant rose gardens; but what most distinguishes *The Wooden Horse* is its passionate adoration of the sea, the cliffs, the weather-worn old Cornish houses, where bearded men tell of haunted moors and the winds of the deep.

"Reading this story after reading his later ones will not prove the disappointment that such a procedure usually is. Here are no signs of faults outgrown, no weaknesses that will hurt the lover of Walpole's later works—by which statement we do not wish to be taken as denying that he has developed. Mr. Walpole is a realist with a wide angle vision to whom not only the littered and close ways of short-sighted and selfish men are real, but to whom the large species of nature and her healing quiet are just as real. He sees life steadily and sees it whole—yet keeps his temper and his hopes."—Llwellyn Jones in *The Chicago Evening Post*.

"Nowhere has Walpole shown a greater grip upon life's realities, a stronger appreciation of the elusiveness of man-made conventionalities and a better artistic sense of the dramatic value of contrasts. In describing the subtle changes brought about in the family circle by the presence of one outside influence, Walpole has displayed much skill and literary power. There are no long disquisitions, no democratic preachments, but his dramatic personæ, when brought face to face with new situations, are moved to action according to their light. This is one of the very best novels from the pen of Mr.

HUGH WALPOLE

Walpole, and that is saying much."—*Philadelphia Public Ledger*.

"A most notable piece of artistry. In Harry Trojan, the 'unrepentant prodigal,' Mr. Walpole has given us a splendid vigorous personality whose acquaintance is a delight to readers wearied by heroes of the type of Harry's semidecadent son. The picture of the Trojan family is one which for vividness could scarcely be surpassed. And, indeed, Mr. Walpole has scarcely written anything more excellent than the account of the dying of Sir Jeremy Trojan—'I am going, but I don't regret anything—your sins are experience—and the greatest sin of all is not having any.' That, in a sense, is the motto of the book. *The Wooden Horse* is one of the few novels which not only may be read, but must be read by the discriminating reader."—*Providence Journal*.

"If one wishes to read a good story without being preached at, he can do no better than read *The Wooden Horse*. The story catches the atmosphere of the Cornish coast, and you have the feel of the salt spray in your nostrils as you read."—*Indianapolis News*.

"As delicate a piece of work as any modern novelist has attempted and superlatively well done."—*Lexington Kentucky Herald*.

HUGH WALPOLE
THE GODS AND MR. PERRIN

HUGH WALPOLE spent some time as a master at an English provincial school, and consequently he has been able to put into *The Gods and Mr. Perrin* quite all the atmosphere of a school where the system, the confinement, the routine of petty tasks get on everyone's nerves and turn a group of human beings into strange hybrids that are at once machines and animals with raw nerves sticking out all over them. Whoever has—whether in the confinement of a school or an unhappy office or a jarring household—been smothered by the atmosphere of some set of human beings, will find himself in this book, and rejoice with Perrin's fight to break free.

The Gods and Mr. Perrin finds Mr. Perrin coming back to the workhouse-like school for boys at the beginning of term-time, determined to be kind this year. But the drudgery, the smell of cold mutton and chalk, the endless succession of frightened boys, the smug ironies of the reverend head-master, get on his nerves, and then the Cat of Cruelty begins to whisper at his ear and suggest that it would be pleasant to twist one boy's ear and cuff another.

He bursts out, at last, gloriously, and at a solemn gathering of the school for the awarding of prizes, tells what he really thinks of the hypocritical headmaster and the drab futility of the whole school.

HUGH WALPOLE

Uncompromisingly, unflinchingly, Walpole has painted that school as it is. His picture should be enough to make any head-master who still believes in education by repression go off and commit suicide. It should be enough to make any man who is yearly growing more choked, more afraid of life, more smothered in a stuffy environment, rebel and fight his way out of that kingdom of dullness, cost what it may.

But because of that very spirit of revolt, *The Gods and Mr. Perrin* is not a drably disagreeable novel which will frighten off soft-minded readers.

"Marked by technical excellence, insight, imagination, and beauty—Walpole at his best."—*San Francisco Bulletin*.

"The psychological crisis in the life of a schoolmaster, uncouth, unhappy and unloved, is keenly analyzed by the hand of a master. The hysteria that attacks the faculty of a boys' school at examination time has never been so well described as in the moving chronicle of the 'Battle of the Umbrella' which proves that Mr. Walpole has the crowning gift of humor."—*The Independent*.

THE PRELUDE TO ADVENTURE

SO excellent is the versatility of Hugh Walpole that this writer of dignified and realistic and always beautiful pictures of life has among his books one with all the tension and strange plot of a Poe

HUGH WALPOLE

masterpiece—*The Prelude to Adventure.* It starts with a murder. Dune the silent, the cleverest yet laziest and most snobbish man in his class at Cambridge, has struck down a red-faced, silly, ignoble, beast of an undergraduate who has been boasting of his conquest over a poor little shopgirl. He did not mean to do murder, but there lay the man dead, where the gray Druids' Wood dripped with rain and gray twilight.

He calmly went back to his rooms and kept silent. What happened is so filled with suspense that, very real and human though it is, the plot comes to have all the unexpectedness of the cleverest detective story. And Dune's vision of God, as a great gray spirit standing gigantic there on the campus, waiting, waiting, is a revelation in spiritual motives. Dune's love story, too, is fascinating—and his victory.

Suspense—color of life—love—fear—triumph—they all mingle in an atmosphere as effective as the Cornish sea.

"A powerful novel of Cambridge life, or rather the story of a Cambridge student with the university sketched in with rapid and sure strokes as a place through which Dune's tragic and lonely figure moves. The sentiment is lofty and manly—Hugh Walpole walks with a sure and firm tread toward a definite goal."—*The Independent.*

HUGH WALPOLE
MARADICK AT FORTY

THE theme of *Maradick at Forty* again gets into the life of every man and every woman; a theme equally timely in 1000 B.C., 1000 A.D. and 10000 A.D.—the question of what is to be done when a man wakes up to find himself getting almost old, with life slipping from him to the next generation. One may smile at the white slave terror, and be quite selfish as regards educational movements, but one cannot smile away the progress of one's self from the forties into the fifties.

Maradick, strong, large, well-bred, a capable stock broker, awakes at forty to find that life has eluded him. He has married respectably—his fussy little wife does not love him. His children are dutiful—they are not admiring. His business is safe—it is not absorbing.

While spending the summer at the "Man at Arms," that marvelous dark old inn with unexpected bits of gardens and tower rooms rambling over the Cornwall cliffs and fronting a vast sweep of sea and sky, he meets with a young man to whom life and poetry are real, to whom women and seas are "bully! marvelous!" The youngster's youth stirs Maradick to demand that he no longer be taken for granted by wife and children and business—and life! He plunges into a spiritual adventure which is the Adventure of Everyman.

THE NOVELS OF HUGH WALPOLE

THE SECRET CITY	*Net $1.75*
THE DARK FOREST	*Net $1.50*
JEREMY	*Net $1.75*
THE GOLDEN SCARECROW	*Net $1.50*
THE GREEN MIRROR	*Net $1.75*
THE DUCHESS OF WREXE	*Net $1.75*
FORTITUDE	*Net $1.75*
THE PRELUDE TO ADVENTURE	*Net $1.50*
MARADICK AT FORTY	*Net $1.50*
THE GODS AND MR. PERRIN	*Net $1.50*
THE WOODEN HORSE	*Net $1.50*

GEORGE H. DORAN COMPANY, *Publishers*
244 Madison Avenue   NEW YORK